Jefferson County
Box N Court Street
Louisville, 40202
(502) 574-6345

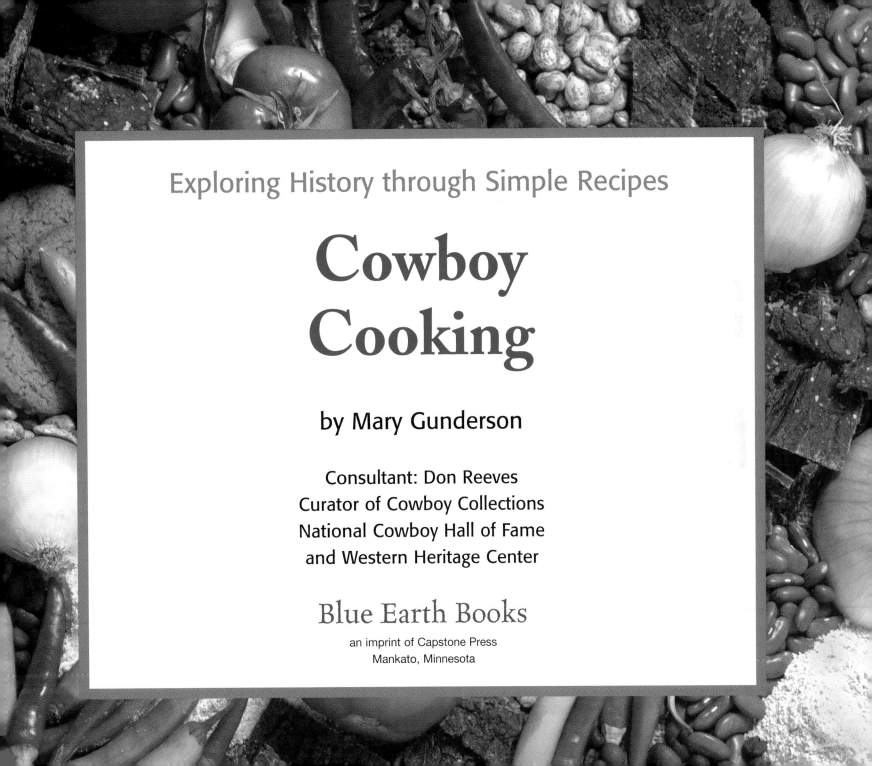

Exploring History through Simple Recipes

Cowboy Cooking

by Mary Gunderson

Consultant: Don Reeves
Curator of Cowboy Collections
National Cowboy Hall of Fame
and Western Heritage Center

Blue Earth Books

an imprint of Capstone Press
Mankato, Minnesota

Blue Earth Books are published by Capstone Press
151 Good Counsel Drive, P.O. Box 669, Mankato, Minnesota 56002
http://www.capstone-press.com

Library of Congress Cataloging-in-Publication Data
Gunderson, Mary.
   Cowboy Cooking / by Mary Gunderson.
   p. cm.—(Exploring history through simple recipes)
   Includes bibliographical references (p. 30) and index.
   Summary: Discusses the everyday life, cooking methods, and common foods of cowboys who moved cattle across the American West in the late
nineteenth century. Includes recipes.
   ISBN 0-7368-0353-X
   1. Cookery, American—Western style—History Juvenile literature. 2. Food habits—West (U.S.)—History—19th century Juvenile literature.
3. Cowboys—West (U.S.)—History—19th century Juvenile literature. [1. Cookery, American—Western style—History. 2. Food habits—West
(U.S.)—History—19th century. 3. Cowboys. 4. West (U.S.)—Social life and customs.] I. Title. II. Series.
TX715.2.W47G87 2000
394.1'0978'09034—dc21
                                                                                                    99-24617
                                                                                                    CIP

Editorial credits
Editors, Rebecca Glaser, Rachel Koestler; cover designer, Steve
Christensen; interior designer, Heather Kindseth; illustrator, Linda
Clavel; photo researcher, Kimberly Danger

Acknowledgments
Blue Earth Books thanks the following children who helped test recipes:
John Christensen, Matthew Christensen, Maerin Coughlan, Beth
Goebel, Nicole Hilger, Abby Rothenbuehler, Alice Ruff, Hannah
Schoof, and Molly Wandersee.

Photo credits
Kansas State Historical Society, cover, 11, 22-23, 23 (inset), 24-25;
Gregg Andersen, cover (background) and recipes, 13, 17, 21, 27, 29;
Library of Congress, 9; National Cowboy Hall of Fame and Western
Heritage Center, 29; Wyoming Division of Cultural Resources, 6, 10,
12, 14-15, 18, 20, 26-27

Editor's note
Adult supervision may be needed for some recipes in this book. All
recipes have been tested. Although based on historical foods, recipes have
been modernized and simplified for today's young cooks.

1 2 3 4 5 6 05 04 03 02 01 00

Contents

Cooking Help

Recipes

References

Metric Conversion Guide

U.S.	Canada
¼ teaspoon	1 mL
½ teaspoon	2 mL
1 teaspoon	5 mL
1 tablespoon	15 mL
¼ cup	50 mL
⅓ cup	75 mL
½ cup	125 mL
⅔ cup	150 mL
¾ cup	175 mL
1 cup	250 mL
1 quart	1 liter
1 ounce	30 grams
2 ounces	55 grams
4 ounces	85 grams
½ pound	225 grams
1 pound	455 grams

Fahrenheit	Celsius
325 degrees	160 degrees
350 degrees	180 degrees
375 degrees	190 degrees
400 degrees	200 degrees
425 degrees	220 degrees

Kitchen Safety

1. Make sure your hair and clothes will not be in the way while you are cooking.

2. Keep a fire extinguisher in the kitchen. Never put water on a grease fire.

3. Wash your hands with soap before you start to cook. Wash your hands with soap again after you handle meat or poultry.

4. Ask an adult for help with sharp knives, the stove, the oven, and all electrical appliances.

5. Turn handles of pots and pans to the middle of the stove. A person walking by could run into handles that stick out toward the room.

6. Use dry pot holders to take dishes out of the oven.

7. Wash all fruits and vegetables.

8. Always use a clean cutting board. Wash the cutting board thoroughly after cutting meat or poultry.

9. Wipe up spills immediately.

10. Store leftovers properly. Do not leave leftovers out at room temperature for more than two hours.

Cooking Equipment

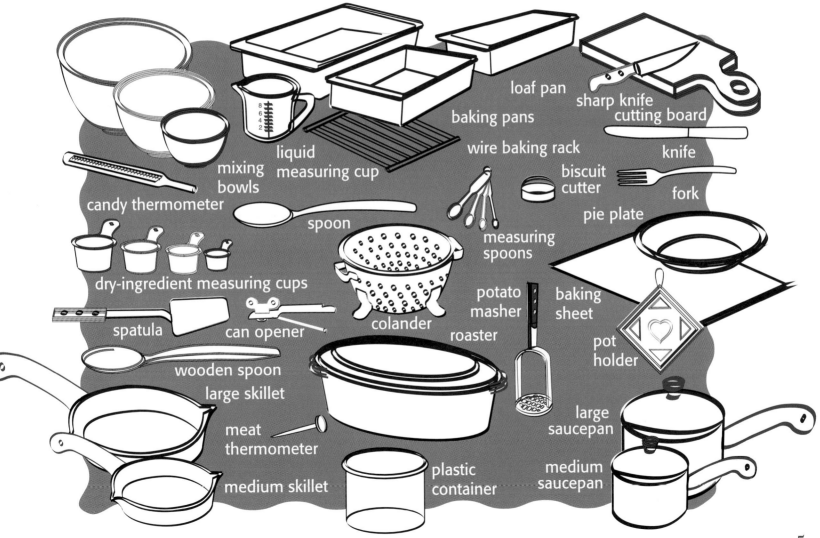

mixing bowls

liquid measuring cup

loaf pan

baking pans

sharp knife

cutting board

wire baking rack

knife

candy thermometer

biscuit cutter

fork

spoon

pie plate

measuring spoons

dry-ingredient measuring cups

colander

potato masher

baking sheet

spatula

can opener

roaster

pot holder

wooden spoon

large skillet

large saucepan

meat thermometer

medium skillet

plastic container

medium saucepan

Roundups and Trail Drives

Cowboys were skilled horsemen who knew how to ride horses, herd cattle, and stop a stampede. They worked on the vast plains of the western United States in the late 1800s. Cowboys came from many backgrounds. Some cowboys were Texans, former Civil War soldiers, former slaves, American Indians, or Mexicans. The average age of a cowboy was 24 years old.

Many cowboys found work in Texas, where ranchers had settled on large areas of land. Texas had room for thousands of cattle to graze on its grassy plains. But Texas was far away from the profitable cattle markets in the north. Ranchers could sell their cattle for $40 each in northern markets. In Texas, cattle brought only $4 each.

In the mid-1800s, there was no easy way to transport large herds of cattle to the higher-paying markets. The closest railroads to Texas were in Missouri and Kansas. Ranch owners hired cowboys to drive herds of cattle to towns in these states and farther north. From these cowtowns, cattle were sold and shipped by railroad to slaughterhouses.

Before cowboys could drive herds north, they had to round up the cattle. In the 1860s and 1870s, ranches did not have fences. During the winter, ranchers let their cattle graze and roam free on the range. Herds from many ranches mixed together. During roundups, cowboys brought all the cattle to one place.

During the fall roundup, cowboys branded calves born in the summer and returned stray cattle to their owners.

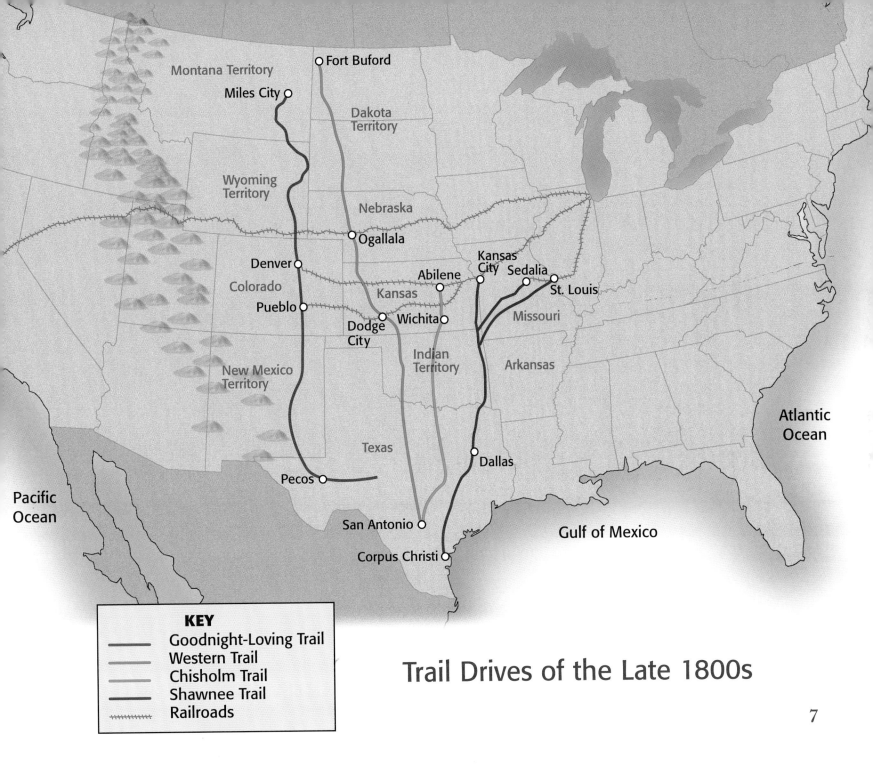

Trail Drives of the Late 1800s

KEY
Goodnight-Loving Trail
Western Trail
Chisholm Trail
Shawnee Trail
Railroads

7

Ranchers organized two roundups each year. These roundups took place in the spring and in the fall. Cowboys from the different ranches set up a roundup camp. They rode the range in surrounding areas and herded the cattle into one large herd near the camp. During the roundup, cowboys moved the herd daily so the cattle could find fresh grass to eat.

After they gathered the cattle, cowboys separated the herds. Brands identified the owners of the cattle. These marks burned into a cow's hide represented the owner's ranch. Another form of identification was ear marks. The ears of cattle, clipped in a certain shape, were easier to spot in a large herd. When the herds were separated and ready to sell, cowboys started driving the cattle north.

In the 1880s, a crew of about 12 men drove a herd more than 1,000 miles (1,600 kilometers) to northern cowtowns. An average crew included a trail boss, eight drivers, a horse wrangler, and a cook. The trail boss was in charge of how far the crew traveled each day. He decided where to set up camp for the night. Cowboys rode alongside the herd and kept the cattle together. The horse wrangler kept track of the remuda, a large group of horses the cowboys used during the trail drive. Cowboys changed horses two to three times a day so the horses did not become tired. The cook was in charge of making all the meals.

Cowboys moved cattle an average of 15 to 20 miles (24 to 32 kilometers) each day. On a trail drive, the speed depended on how fast the cattle could walk. The speed also depended on how often the cowboys let cattle stop to eat grass and drink water.

Cowboys worked hard. They took breaks only for meals and to sleep. Cowboys had to work whether it was hot, windy, raining, or cold. If the food was good, the cowboys had that pleasure, at least.

In the late 1800s, cowboys drove thousands of cattle to market from dawn until dusk. They camped each night, sleeping outdoors on bedrolls.

Chuck Wagon Cooks

T he chuck wagon was a daily part of cowboy life. From this moveable kitchen, the cook served two or three hot meals to a crew of cowboys every day.

The cook often was an older man who had been a cowboy. He was no longer quick enough for the hard and sometimes dangerous work with cattle. "Cookie" often was his nickname. Some cowboys called the cook "Belly Cheater," "Dough Puncher," or "Biscuit Shooter." But they always called him "Mister" to his face.

The cook was second in command to the trail boss. Cowboys respected him. No one took anything from the chuck wagon without the cook's permission. Cowboys knew they might receive less food if they made the cook angry.

The ranch owner hired the cook and supplied the food. Cookie had to make the best of the ingredients he was given. If the ranch owner was generous, food was plentiful. The cook sometimes even had ingredients for treats like cookies or pies.

Each day, the trail boss rode ahead and found a place to camp. He chose a spot near water, usually by a creek or a river. The cook followed the trail boss in the chuck wagon. Cookie set up the new campsite.

The cook dug a hole in the ground and built a fire in it. The cook often used dried cow droppings for campfire fuel because wood was scarce. Few trees grew on the grass-covered prairie. Cowboys called dried cow droppings "prairie coal." After starting the fire, the cook set up iron stakes with a crossbar to hang pots over the fire.

Chuck wagon cooks called cowboys to each meal. Cookie yelled "Come and get it," "Chuck away,'" or "Grub pile. This cook probably worked for a ranch in the 1930s.

The chuck wagon had a tall cupboard called a chuck box attached to the back. Lightweight items such as utensils, dishes, and spices sat in the top part of the chuck box. Food held in tin canisters, wooden kegs and boxes, cloth bags, and pottery crocks filled the middle part of the chuck box. Cooks stored heavier items such as iron pots and pans in a box bolted underneath the wagon. The cover of a chuck box folded down and rested on a fold-out leg to make a table.

Cookie kept more supplies in the wagon itself. Chuck wagons held up to a 30-day supply of food. They carried flour, coffee, beans, sugar, molasses, lard, canned goods, and dried fruit. The wagon also held horseshoes, medical items, and bedrolls. A barrel on the side of the wagon held 35 gallons (132 liters) of water. That amount was enough water to last 11 cowboys and a cook two days. The cook refilled the water barrel from creeks and rivers.

Airtights

Cowboys called cans of food "airtights." Any vegetables or fruits cowboys ate on the trail were canned or dried. There was no way to keep fruits or vegetables fresh during trail drives. On the trail, cowboys often drank canned tomato juice when the water was bad. Canned peaches were a favorite treat on the trail. The cowboys sometimes drank canned milk, which they called "canned cow."

During roundups, some cooks prepared food for more than 40 cowboys.

The Dutch Oven

The Dutch oven was the most important piece of equipment in the chuck wagon. Cookie used the Dutch oven as a frying pan, mini-oven, stew pot, pie tin, and cake pan. The chuck wagon stored several sizes of these pots. Cookie sometimes used all of them to make a meal.

Dutch ovens were made of thick cast iron. These black pots were 10 to 20 inches (25 to 51 centimeters) around and weighed up to 30 pounds (14 kilograms). Dutch ovens were almost impossible to chip, crack, or break. Each pot was about 4 inches (10 centimeters) deep and had three or four short legs. A heavy wire handle made the pot easy to hang over a fire and easy to carry from the fire.

Dutch oven lids fit tightly to hold in steam and heat during cooking. The lid edges curved upward so that hot coals could be placed on top of the pots. A lid placed upside-down over a fire became a grill.

Cooks controlled the temperature of Dutch ovens by placing them in different locations by the fire. They set Dutch ovens directly over the fire or in the fire to cook at hot temperatures. To cook at lower temperatures, cooks set Dutch ovens on hot coals spread on the ground. For even cooking, they lined hot coals on the lid.

Cookie used a Dutch oven to make cornmeal mush and corn dodgers. He mixed cornmeal and water in a Dutch oven. He hung the pot over the fire to boil. The cornmeal thickened into mush. The next day, Cookie often cut leftover cornmeal mush into squares called corn dodgers. He fried the dodgers in lard in the Dutch oven.

Cowboys filed through a chuck line. They filled their plates and cups directly from the pots and skillets.

Cornmeal Mush

Ingredients
2¾ cups water
1¾ cups cornmeal
1 cup cold water
1 tablespoon firmly packed
  brown sugar
1 teaspoon salt
butter and syrup, as desired

Equipment
medium saucepan
liquid measuring cup
dry-ingredient measuring
  cups
measuring spoons
medium bowl
wooden spoon

1. In saucepan, bring 2¾ cups water to a boil.
2. Meanwhile, mix 1¾ cups cornmeal, 1 cup cold water, 1 tablespoon brown sugar, and 1 teaspoon salt in bowl.
3. Slowly add mixture to boiling water, stirring constantly.
4. Cook over low heat about 15 minutes until thickened, stirring often.
5. Save half of mixture for corn dodgers.
6. Serve remaining mush with butter and syrup.

Makes 6 servings.

Corn Dodgers

Ingredients
1 tablespoon butter or
  margarine for greasing
½ recipe cornmeal mush
1 tablespoon oil for frying

Equipment
paper towel or napkin
loaf pan, 5-inch by 9-inch
  (13-centimeter by
  23-centimeter)
table knife
cutting board
measuring spoons
skillet or electric skillet
spatula

1. Grease loaf pan by using paper towel or napkin to dab and spread 1 tablespoon of butter or margarine to lightly coat inside of pan.
2. Pour cornmeal mush into loaf pan.
3. Chill several hours or overnight.
4. Loosen cornmeal from sides of pan with table knife and turn out onto cutting board.
5. Cut into ½-inch (1.3-centimeter) slices.
6. Heat 1 tablespoon oil in skillet.
7. Fry cornmeal slices over low heat. Turn once. Fry until browned, 4 to 5 minutes on each side.
8. Serve with gravy or with butter and syrup.

Makes 6 servings.

Biscuits at Every Meal

ookie made biscuits once or twice each day. He served biscuits with almost every meal and had to make large batches of them. One cook wrote that his cowboys each ate 11 biscuits at a single meal.

Cooks made different kinds of biscuits. Cowboys liked hot, tender biscuits best. Sourdough biscuits were a favorite. Cowboys welcomed the rich, tangy flavor of these biscuits. They called sourdough biscuits names such as "sinkers," "hot rocks," and "dough gods."

Cookie made sourdough biscuits from flour, water, sourdough starter, baking powder, and salt. He usually did not have eggs or milk on the trail. Sourdough starter was a mixture of flour, water, and a little fermented sugar. Cookie added water and flour to the starter to equal the amount he took out. That way, he never ran out of sourdough starter. Some cooks also used sourdough starter for pies, puddings, dumplings, cinnamon rolls, and doughnuts.

The fire pit was too hot for baking biscuits. Instead, Cookie lifted hot coals out of the fire and laid them close together on the ground. He placed the covered Dutch oven on top of the coals and set more hot coals on the curved lid. The slow heat from the top and bottom of the Dutch oven baked biscuits evenly. When the biscuits were golden brown, the cowboys lined up to eat.

"Our first meal was dry salt bacon, strong coffee, biscuits about the size of silver dollars, five inches high, real light, crusted over with sugar."

Oliver Nelson, 1880

Biscuits were such a large part of the cowboy diet that "Rollout and bite the biscuit" became a cowboy call to breakfast.

Sourdough Starter

Cowboy cooks always kept sourdough starter on hand. You will need to make sourdough starter one or two days before making biscuits. The sourdough biscuit dough needs to rise overnight before baking.

Ingredients
2 cups water
1 package active dry
   yeast (2¼ teaspoons)
2 cups all-purpose flour

Equipment
liquid measuring cup
saucepan
candy thermometer
large bowl
wooden spoon
plastic wrap

1. Heat 2 cups water to about 110°F (43°C). Check temperature with candy thermometer.
2. Pour into large bowl. Dissolve yeast in water. Let stand about 10 minutes, until bubbly.
3. Gradually add 2 cups of flour to water, stirring often.
4. Cover bowl loosely with plastic wrap.
5. Let stand at room temperature 24 to 48 hours, stirring occasionally.

Coffee

Cookie always had a pot of coffee ready first thing in the morning. The cook often had to build up the fire and start cooking as early as 3:30 a.m. Cowboys went to work before the sun rose.

To make coffee, Cookie put several handfuls of coffee grounds in a large coffee pot full of water. He hung the pot near the fire to boil.

Coffee was the cowboys' favorite drink. They drank coffee with every meal. They liked coffee black, with no cream or sugar. Cowboys often softened hard biscuits by dunking them in the coffee.

Sourdough Biscuits

Ingredients

¼ cup sourdough starter
½ cup water or milk
1¼ to 1½ cups all-purpose flour
2 teaspoons granulated sugar
½ cup whole-wheat flour
½ teaspoon baking powder
¼ teaspoon baking soda
¼ teaspoon salt
1 tablespoon butter or margarine

Equipment

liquid measuring cup
saucepan
candy thermometer
2 medium bowls
dry-ingredient measuring cups
clean dish towel
measuring spoons
wooden spoon
cutting board
biscuit cutter or round drinking glass
cake pan, 9 inches by 13 inches (23 centimeters by 33 centimeters)
pastry brush
wire baking rack
pot holders

The Night Before

1. Heat ½ cup water in saucepan to about 110°F (43 °C). Check temperature with candy thermometer.
2. In one medium bowl, mix ¼ cup sourdough starter, water and ½ cup all-purpose flour. Cover with towel. Set in warm place 70°F to 80°F (21°C to 27°C) overnight.

The Next Day

1. Preheat oven to 375°F.
2. In other bowl, mix ¾ cup all-purpose flour, 2 teaspoons sugar, ½ cup whole-wheat flour, ½ teaspoon baking powder, ¼ teaspoon baking soda, and ¼ teaspoon salt.
3. Stir into starter mixture until smooth.
4. Turn dough out on floured cutting board, adding small amounts of all-purpose flour to form a soft dough.
5. Press dough into a 4-inch by 9-inch (10-centimeter by 23-centimeter) rectangle, about ½-inch (1.3 centimeters) thick. Dip biscuit cutter or drinking glass in flour. Press cutter or glass into dough to make round biscuits.
6. Re-roll dough scraps. Cut biscuits.
7. Drop 1 tablespoon butter into cake pan. Place into oven to melt the butter. After butter is melted, use a pastry brush to spread melted butter over bottom of cake pan.
8. Place biscuits in pan.
9. Cover with damp towel and let rise in warm place 30 minutes.
10. Bake for 25 to 30 minutes, or until slightly browned.
11. Cool on wire baking rack.   Makes about 8 biscuits

Beans, Again and Again

Cowboys expected beans on the menu almost every day. Cooks served beans as a side dish to any kind of food. Cowboys ate beans with biscuits and gravy, with cornbread, and with beef.

Cookie always stocked a supply of pinto beans in the chuck wagon. These dried beans do not spoil easily. They were easy to store in the chuck wagon. Beans provided protein, which gave the cowboys energy for hard work.

Beans tasted best when cooked with spices, fat, meat, or vegetables. Some cowboy cooks added hot chile peppers to their beans. They often cooked bacon with beans. Beef fat or lard gave extra flavor to beans.

Dried beans took a long time to cook. Beans needed to soak up water to become soft. Cookie started cooking beans right after breakfast. He mixed the ingredients in a Dutch oven hanging over a hot fire. After the mixture boiled, he put on the lid. He packed the hot Dutch oven in the chuck wagon. The oven held in heat to cook the beans while Cookie traveled to the next campsite.

Some cowboy crews had Mexican cooks. They made refried beans for the cowboys. This dish was popular in southern Texas near the Mexican border. To make refried beans, cooks boiled pinto beans, mashed them, and added spices and bacon.

After the evening meal, cowboys exchanged stories and recalled past trail drives. Cowboys sometimes had a dance during large roundups.

Refried Beans

This recipe calls for red pepper. Red pepper is spicy. If you do not like spicy food, add just a pinch between your thumb and forefinger.

Ingredients
1 medium onion
4 slices bacon
2 (16-ounce) cans pinto beans
1 tablespoon cumin
1 teaspoon oregano
1/8 teaspoon ground red (cayenne) pepper
1/2 teaspoon salt

Equipment
cutting board
sharp knife
large skillet
colander
2 medium bowls
can opener
potato masher or fork
measuring spoons
wooden spoon

1. Remove skin from onion. Chop onion into small pieces.
2. Cut 4 slices bacon into 1/2-inch (1.3-centimeter) pieces.
3. In skillet, cook onion and bacon over medium-high heat 4 minutes until onion is very tender.
4. Put colander in bowl. Drain beans in colander. Save bean liquid. Put beans in second bowl. Mash.
5. Stir 1 tablespoon cumin, 1 teaspoon oregano, 1/8 teaspoon ground red pepper, and 1/2 teaspoon salt into onion mixture.
6. Add mashed beans and 2 tablespoons of bean liquid.
7. Reduce heat to very low. Continue to mash beans with a fork until there are no large bean pieces left. Cook uncovered, stirring frequently, about 30 minutes or until beans thicken and are still moist. Add a little bean liquid if beans become dry.

Makes 6 servings.

19

The Cowboy Appetite for Meat

Cowboys liked to eat meat. The cattle crews preferred beef. Owners usually limited the number of cattle the cowboys could eat. They lost money if the crew ate too many cattle. Cowboys also ate salt pork, bacon, and wild game. They hunted deer, elk, antelope, squirrel, buffalo, or bear, depending on where they camped.

When beef was allowed, the cook butchered an animal from the herd. He carved out steaks from the tender parts of the animal. Cookie grilled steaks on an upside-down Dutch oven lid. He cut tough meat into cubes for chili and stew. He cut some of the meat into strips and dried it with salt and spices to make beef jerky. Cowboys snacked on jerky while they worked.

"Son-of-a-gun" stew was a cowboy specialty. This dish contained the heart, lungs, and other organs from the animal, plus seasonings. Cookie let the stew simmer for at least 3 hours in a Dutch oven.

Southwestern cooks also made chili in a Dutch oven. They never added beans to their chili. This cowboy chili contained chunks of beef, tomatoes, and seasonings.

Cowboy cooks used pots, kettles, skillets, and ovens to cook meat. They grilled steaks, simmered meat cubes in stew, and dried salted beef for jerky.

Beef Chili

Ingredients

1 large onion
4 slices bacon
1 pound cubed lean beef
(round or chuck steak)
½ teaspoon garlic powder
1 tablespoon ground cumin
2 teaspoons dried oregano leaves,
crushed

½ teaspoon salt
¼ teaspoon pepper
¼ teaspoon ground red (cayenne)
pepper
1 (28-ounce) can diced tomatoes,
undrained
1 (14- to 16-ounce) can beef broth
2 tablespoons yellow cornmeal

Equipment

cutting board
sharp knife
Dutch oven or large saucepan
wooden spoon
measuring spoons
can opener

1. Remove peel from onion. Chop onion into small pieces.
2. Cut 4 slices bacon into ½-inch (1.3-centimeter) pieces.
3. In Dutch oven or saucepan, cook onion and bacon over
   medium-high heat for 4 minutes, stirring occasionally.
4. Cut 1 pound beef into bite-sized chunks.
5. Add beef, ½ teaspoon garlic powder, 1 tablespoon cumin,
   2 teaspoons oregano, ½ teaspoon salt, ¼ teaspoon pepper, and
   ¼ teaspoon red pepper to onion and bacon. Red pepper is
   spicy. If you do not like spicy food, you may wish to add just a
   pinch between your thumb and forefinger. Mix well.
6. Cook and stir about 5 minutes.
7. Add tomatoes and juice from can. Add beef broth. Stir. Reduce
   heat. Cook uncovered at least 30 minutes, stirring occasionally.
8. Add 2 tablespoons cornmeal. Stir. Cook 15 minutes longer or
   until chili is slightly thickened.

Makes about 8 servings.

21

Cowboy Clothing: Fit for Work

Cowboys needed comfortable, sturdy clothes when they were riding. They wore loose-fitting cotton or flannel shirts and thick canvas or woolen pants. Cowboys wore vests with pockets, because it was hard for them to reach pockets in pants while riding horseback. Chaps protected cowboys' legs. These leather leggings wrapped around the legs and fastened in back. In the north, cowboys sometimes wore heavy jackets to protect their arms.

Cowboy boots had rounded toes so a cowboy's foot could slide easily into the stirrup. Thick heels on the boots kept the feet from sliding too far into the stirrups. Spurs were spiked wheels attached to cowboy boots. Cowboys pressed spurs into horses' sides to make them run faster.

A bandanna was one of the most important items of clothing a cowboy wore. Cowboys tied these square pieces of cloth around their necks. A bandanna could be tied over the face as a dust mask or used as a sling or bandage in case of injury. Cowboys also used bandannas as a washcloth and towel, or to blindfold a horse to calm it.

No cowboy was completely dressed without his hat. The wide brim of a cowboy hat shielded the face from sun and rain. Cowboys might use a hat to fan a campfire or dip water to drink. Cowboys also used their hats to get the attention of others. A cowboy waving his hat could be seen from a long distance.

Cowboy Manners

Despite a rough life with few comforts, cowboys followed an unwritten code of hospitality. On a trail drive, any stranger could join the cowboys for a meal. No questions were asked. The stranger was free to tell or not to tell his name, where he came from, or where he was going.

Cowboys and their guests sat on the ground to eat. A cowboy held his plate in his lap. He did not wait for others to be served. He started to eat as soon as the food was on the plate. A cowboy could put as much food as he wanted on his plate. But he was expected to eat everything he took.

While outdoors, cowboys ate with their hats on. That was polite. Indoors, they took off their hats.

A cowboy was always careful to keep dust away from the food. No one saddled or unsaddled a horse near the chuck wagon. Only a "greenhorn," or a new cowboy, would ride his horse into camp upwind of the chuck wagon and campfire. The wind would stir up dust that would get into the food.

It was considered polite to wipe up leftovers on the plate with a biscuit. Gravy, which cowboys called "dough sop," helped the food bits stick to the biscuit. When cowboys were done eating, they put their dishes in a huge dishpan under the chuck box lid.

Breakfast or lunch was no time for chatter. As soon as the trail boss finished eating, cowboys had to be ready to ride out on the trail.

24

Beef and Gravy

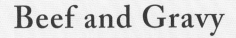

Ingredients

1 4- to 6-pound (1.8- to 2.7-kilogram)
  top round roast
½ cup water
¼ cup all-purpose flour
1 cup beef broth
⅛ teaspoon salt
⅛ teaspoon pepper

Equipment

shallow roasting pan
meat thermometer
cutting board
pot holders
liquid measuring cup
wooden spoon
plastic container with lid
can opener
measuring spoons
sharp knife

1. Preheat oven to 325°F.
2. Place meat with fat side up in shallow roasting pan. Insert meat thermometer so tip is in center of roast. Do not let thermometer tip touch bone or fat.
3. Roast, uncovered.
4. Check meat after 1 hour. Remove meat from oven when the meat thermometer reads 155°F (137°C) for medium, or 170°F (152°C) for well done. Meat will continue to cook after it is removed from oven.
5. Place roast on cutting board. Let roast stand 15 to 20 minutes for easier carving.
6. Add ½ cup water to roasting pan. Bring mixture to boil on stove. Stir and scrape meat and drippings from pan. Remove from heat.
7. In a plastic container with lid, combine ¼ cup flour and 1 cup cold beef broth. Secure lid and shake well to mix.
8. Pour mixture into drippings and bring to boil.
9. Add ⅛ teaspoon salt and ⅛ teaspoon pepper. Cook 2 to 3 minutes or until mixture thickens, stirring often.
10. Have an adult help cut the roast. Serve with gravy.

Serves 6 to 8. Makes about 2 cups gravy.

Treats for the Cowboy Sweet Tooth

Cooks sometimes made desserts for the cowboys. After eating the same foods day after day, the cowboys welcomed a sweet treat. Cowboys enjoyed a dish of apple cobbler or a gingersnap. Bread puddings also were common.

Cowboy cooks rarely had fresh ingredients such as eggs or milk. Sugar was rare too. If cooks had sugar, it was brown sugar, which quickly became hard. Cooks used molasses as a sweetener because it was plentiful and inexpensive.

Cookie often made fruit desserts. These dishes were the cowboys' favorite treat. Cookie often had dried apples, dried prunes, or raisins. The cook occasionally had canned peaches on hand. In the late summer, Cookie sent his helpers out to find wild berries or sand plums. Cookie baked these fruits with biscuit dough. He sometimes baked dough on top of fruit sauce. Other times, he wrapped the fruit inside biscuit dough.

Gingersnaps were another common dessert. Cooks used molasses to sweeten these hard cookies. Cooks sometimes kept bags of gingersnaps in the chuck wagon. Gingersnaps did not spoil as quickly as other cookies. Cowboys could take a handful for snacks on the trail.

Cooks baked desserts with wild berries found along streams. They sweetened these desserts with brown sugar or molasses before baking them in a Dutch oven.

Gingersnaps

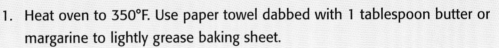

Ingredients

1 tablespoon butter or margarine
  for greasing
1 cup granulated sugar
¾ cup butter or margarine, softened
1 egg
¼ cup molasses
2 cups all-purpose flour
2 teaspoons baking soda
2 teaspoons ground ginger
1 teaspoon cinnamon
½ teaspoon cloves
½ teaspoon nutmeg
¼ cup granulated sugar

Equipment

paper towel
large bowl
electric mixer or hand mixer
baking sheet
dry-ingredient measuring cups
electric mixer or hand mixer
wooden spoon
small bowl
small, shallow bowl
pot holders
spatula
wire baking rack

1. Heat oven to 350°F. Use paper towel dabbed with 1 tablespoon butter or margarine to lightly grease baking sheet.

2. Beat 1 cup sugar and ¾ cup butter in large bowl with electric mixer or hand mixer until creamy.

3. Add 1 egg and ¼ cup molasses. Blend until smooth.

4. Combine 2 cups flour, 2 teaspoons baking soda, 2 teaspoons ginger, 1 teaspoon cinnamon, ½ teaspoon cloves, and ½ teaspoon nutmeg in small bowl.

5. Add flour mixture to sugar mixture. Mix until well-blended.

6. Put ¼ cup sugar in shallow bowl. Form dough into 1-inch (2.5-centimeter) balls. Roll dough balls in sugar. Place on baking sheet.

7. Bake about 10 minutes or until golden brown and dry around edges. Cool on wire baking rack.

Makes about 5 dozen cookies.

Fourth of July

In the late 1800s, cowboys usually finished spring roundups and trail drives by the Fourth of July. Cowboys delivered the cattle to railroads or new ranges. Owners paid the cowboys for their work. Cowboys then were free to do what they wanted. Some went home by train, carrying their saddles with them. Some stayed to celebrate in cowtowns like Dodge City and Abilene, Kansas.

Cowtowns were a welcome sight to many cowboys. Most cowboys had been wearing the same clothes for weeks and had bathed only in cold rivers. In town, cowboys could take warm baths, buy new clothes, sleep in comfortable beds, and relax. They spent time in local saloons and restaurants. After being alone on the trail for so long, they welcomed the company of townspeople.

Cowboys joined in Fourth of July celebrations. People ate, drank, and visited. Cowboys often went to box socials. Young women brought their best pies and cakes to the socials. Men bid on the pies and cakes at these auctions. A man could sit with a woman after he had bought her pie or cake.

A cowboy welcomed any kind of fruit pie. Pie always was a treat for cowboys and was a symbol of a more settled life. Good peach pie could get a cowboy's attention at a box social.

The Beginning of the Rodeo

Visitors came to cowtowns from all over the region for the Fourth of July. Cowboys from different crews gathered for what they called "cowboy fun." Cowboys tried to outdo each other with tricks. They showed off their roping skills. They competed to see how long each cowboy could ride a bucking horse. They raced their horses.

These contests were the beginning of the rodeo tradition. Rodeo is the Spanish word for "roundup." Today, cowboys and cowgirls compete in rodeos across the United States and in Canada and Mexico.

Peach Pie

Ingredients

2 (16-ounce) cans sliced peaches
½ cup brown sugar
¼ cup all-purpose flour
¼ teaspoon nutmeg
⅛ teaspoon salt
2 refrigerated pie crusts
1 tablespoon granulated sugar

Equipment

can opener
colander
large bowl
dry-ingredient measuring cups
measuring spoons
wooden spoon
pie plate
fork
sharp knife
pot holders
aluminum foil

1. Preheat oven to 400°F.
2. Drain peaches in colander. Put peaches in bowl.
3. Add ½ cup brown sugar, ¼ cup flour, ¼ teaspoon nutmeg, and ⅛ teaspoon salt. Stir.
4. Place one crust in pie plate. Press against pie plate to shape.
5. Spoon peach mixture into pie crust.
6. Gently place second pie crust over peach mixture. Fold edges of top crust over bottom crust. Press around edge of pie with fork.
7. Cut 4 1-inch (2.5-centimeter), angled slits in crust near center of pie.
8. Sprinkle 1 tablespoon sugar over pie crust.
9. Bake 40-45 minutes or until crust is golden brown and filling is bubbling. Check pie halfway through baking. If crust edges are browning quickly, carefully cover the edges with strips of aluminum foil.

Makes 8 servings.

Words to Know

auction (AWK-shuhn)—a sale at which something is sold to the person who offers the most money for it

ferment (fur-MENT)—a chemical reaction caused when yeast mixes with water and flour; sourdough starter ferments.

greenhorn (GREEN-horn)—a new cowboy

hospitality (hoss-puh-TAL-uh-tee)—showing openness and being friendly to guests

jerky (JURK-ee)—beef seasoned with spices and dried over low heat

range (RAYNJ)—an area of open land used for a special purpose, as in a cattle range

rodeo (ROH-dee-oh)—the Spanish word for "roundup;" this word was adopted by cowboys as a name for competitive events.

roundup (ROWND-uhp)—the time when cowboys gather stray cattle

territory (TER-uh-tor-ee)—an area of the United States that is not yet a state

trail drive (TRAYL DRIVE)—a trip during which cowboys herd hundreds or thousands of cattle across many miles

To Learn More

Cody, Tod. *The Cowboy's Handbook: How to Become a Hero of the Wild West.* New York: Cobblehill Books, 1996.

Erdosh, George. *Food and Recipes of the Westward Expansion.* Cooking throughout American History. New York: PowerKids Press, 1997.

Pelta, Kathy. *Cattle Trails: Git Along Little Dogies.* American Trails. Austin, Texas: Raintree Steck-Vaughn, 1997.

Penner, Lucille Recht. *Cowboys.* All Aboard Books. New York: Grosset & Dunlap, 1996.

Santella, Andrew. *The Chisholm Trail.* Cornerstones of Freedom. New York: Children's Press, 1998.

Wukovits, John F. *The Black Cowboys.* Legends of the West. Broomall, Penn.: Chelsea House, 1997.

Places to Write and Visit

Autry Museum of Western Heritage
4700 Western Heritage Way
Los Angeles, CA 90027-1462

Cowboy Country Museum
113 Wetherbee
Stamford, TX 79553

Buffalo Bill Historical Center
720 Sheridan Avenue
Cody, WY 82414

National Cowboy Hall of Fame
1700 NE 63rd Street
Oklahoma City, OK 73111

Chisholm Trail Historical Museum
Route 2, Box 124
Waurika, OK 73573

National Cowgirl Hall of Fame
111 West 4th Street, Suite 300
Fort Worth, TX 76102

Internet Sites

Along the Chisholm Trail
http://www.texhoma.net/~glencbr/p001.html

Trail Drives of the Old West
http://www.net.westhost.com/trail1.htm

National Cowboy Hall of Fame-Children's Wing
http://www.cowboyhalloffame.org/children.html

The Western Heritage Centre
http://www.whcs.ab.ca/

National Cowgirl Museum and Hall of Fame
http://www.cowgirl.net

Index